DYNAMICS

OF

GOD'S WORD

(How the Word becomes flesh)

Andrew Allans Mutambo.

To order copies online visit: www.andrewmutambo.com

Or by mail contact:

Andrew Allans Mutambo

P.O BOX 22292

Kampala, Uganda.

U.S Line: 1-804-601-0394.

Uganda line: 011-256-77-240-4389

Email: andymutts@gmail.com

Rivendell Publishing

www.rivendellpublishing.com

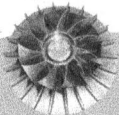

Andrew Allans Mutambo

Dedication

I dedicate this book to my heavenly father and King who through the years has been opening my eyes to snippets of the mysteries of His word and inspiring me to express them on paper; so that my readers may be touched, inspired and transformed through this ministry. For all who occasion to read this book, let this manuscript transform your perception of the Word of God and enable you live your life to the fullest potential.

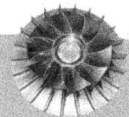

Acknowledgements

My fellow Pastors' in the Vineyard of God, Revived Glory Church, thank you for your continuous encouragement, love, prayers, and allowing me spend time to pursue my authorial dream. To my Church family, my sincere gratitude for your love, support and patience during the times of separation and study in the course of writing my books. Your prayers are always appreciated.

Endorsement

Authoring is a skill and passion only a cross section of writers in Africa pursue. The spiritual ideas we encode in books go far and speak long after we are gone. Andrew is one of those upcoming leaders in the Body of Christ who have heeded the call and decided to run with this conviction. He is a young, apt and dynamic Pastor that God is raising with a cutting edge message for our nation and generation. His witting style is simple and straight forward. His book 'Dynamics of God's Word', offers fresh perspective on how the Word of God operates in and through a yielded Christian life. We all need books that will inspire and prod us to dig deeper into ourselves and climber higher in pursuit of God. This is such a one. It teaches you to be radical and remain real, pragmatic yet perceptive and will provide valuable insights on how to achieve your desired goals. Read it carefully and meditatively.

Dr. Joseph Serwadda.

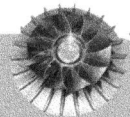

Table of Contents

Dedication i

Acknowledgement ii

Endorsement iii

Table of Contents iv

Preface viii

Chapter 1   Place of the Word 1

Chapter 2   Purpose of the Word 14

Chapter 3   Position of the Word 26

Conclusion 33

Other books written by Andrew Allans Mutambo 37

Books comming soon 37

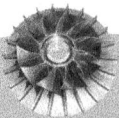

Preface

The Word of God is the oldest and most credible piece of work handed to Man. It's encoded with set bounds and seasons for nations and kingdoms; past, present and future. It is also the greatest spiritual tool that has been availed to His Church and the foremost asset in accessing the voice of God. It's the embodiment of the express mind and will of God.

When it comes to the Kingdom of God, His Word is Law. He rules, governs and administrates by it. Everything that was created is a product of His Word. Because as a king, all He does is but speak. The five days of creation in the book Genesis attest to His power of proclamation. *Hebrews 11:3 Through faith we understand that the worlds were framed by the word of God, so that things which are seen were not made of things which do appear.* When it comes to our lives, through His

Fatherly voice, He speaks our destinies into being. Our healing, deliverance, protection, prosperity and so on. *Psalms 107:20 He sent his word, and healed them, and delivered them from their destructions.* We therefore, as Kingdom Citizens, ought to emulate our king by creating a wholesome 'world' around; as we declare His Word into every affair of our lives.

The Word of God is two bits in one; the written Word (commonly called the Bible) AND the Living Word (the Eternal Christ). Before the express/written Word was, the Living Word was. That is why heaven refers to Christ as the Word of God. *Revelation 19:13 And he was clothed with a vesture dipped in blood: and his name is called The Word of God.*

Through the ages, His written Word has been criticized, ostracized, misused, treaded and burnt; with the hope of making it extinct. It has viciously endured the wrath of emperors, Kings, despotic rulers and religious crusaders. Notwithstanding, it still abides and remains the only credible document that sheds light on the will, purpose, plan and design of God for every unborn, living and dead persons.

Andrew Allans Mutambo

The written Word also known as Logos, is a product of God. Logos means 'reason and thought'. It is God's reasoning and thinking about Man and the universe, His voice through the eon of time. The Word of God carries the breath of His Eternal Spirit upon it. You cannot separate the Living logos from the written logos; because the latter is a product of the former. *John 6:63 It is the spirit that quickeneth; the flesh profiteth nothing: the words that I speak unto you, they are spirit, and they are life.*

Some refer to it as a traveler's map, a pilgrim's staff, a river of pleasure, a mine of wealth, a paradise of glory and a soldier's sword. When put into use, it cuts two ways; capable of both a direct stroke and a back stroke. While bringing conviction to the human soul, it also destroys the devil's works and influence thereby.

Assuming His Word was an immense battle-ship, am going to attempt to sketch a map of it; starting with the interior and side views and making my way to the exterior and elevated views. In this book, Dynamics of God's Word, I communicate the Place, Purpose and Position of

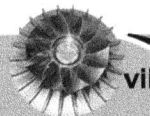

His Word. Through it, I spell out the transforming and working processes of His word from the moment it is received and conceived, through its incubation stage, till it is released to become a formidable weapon. Tag with me as we discover and learn to put to use the greatest arsenal God has availed to His spiritual Army. Our main scriptural reference is drawn from the gospel of John.

John 1:1 In the beginning was the Word, and the Word was with God, and the Word was God.

Chapter One

Place of the Word

The Scripture begins with a primary preposition 'IN' signifying a fixed position; in place, time or state. The writer illustrates the Word as being 'in' NOT besides, beneath, behind or upon. Meaning, throughout the vicissitudes of time, the Word has been 'in the Beginning'. What is the 'beginning'. Astonishingly, God refers to himself as the Beginning! *Revelation 22:13 I am Alpha and Omega, the beginning and the end, the first and the last.* God the father is, the Beginning and source of all things. The Ancient of days. And in His infinite wisdom, chose to place His Word, the Living Christ, deep inside him.

John 1:2 He was in the beginning with God (1889 Darby Bible).

The intimacy and affection the Father and Son have enjoyed from eternity past and present hinge on the fact that Jesus (the Living Word) abides in the bosom of His Father. In this fixed place, an environment that is perfect, conducive and ungoverned by the laws of time; the Living Word thrives. In here the Son enjoys unbroken and unhindered fellowship and friendship. The father chose to 'hide' His Word IN Him because of the worth and value He places on Him.

John 14:11 Believe me that I am in the Father, and the Father in me: or else believe me for the very works' sake.

Correspondingly, as Christians, the placement of God's Word in our lives begins in the way we perceive and receive it into our hearts (spirit-man), which is the innermost section of our temples. This in turn will dictate the spiritual atmosphere for it to thrive and abound.

John 15:7 If ye abide in me, and my words abide in you, ye shall ask what ye will, and it shall be done unto you. John 15:8 Herein is my Father glorified, that ye bear much fruit; so shall ye be my disciples.

We are going to use the following passage as our study guide in helping us understand how the Word makes its entrance.

1Kings 8:1 Then Solomon assembled the elders of Israel, and all the heads of the tribes, the chief of the fathers of the children of Israel, unto king Solomon in Jerusalem, that they might bring up the Ark of the covenant of the LORD out of the city of David, which is Zion.

1Kings 8:2 And all the men of Israel assembled themselves unto king Solomon at the feast in the month Ethanim, which is the seventh month.

1Kings 8:3 And all the elders of Israel came, and the priests took up the Ark.

1Kings 8:4 And they brought up the Ark of the LORD, and the tabernacle of the congregation, and all the holy vessels that were in the tabernacle, even those did the priests and the Levites bring up.

1Kings 8:5 And king Solomon, and all the congregation of Israel, that were assembled unto him, were with him before the Ark, sacrificing sheep and oxen, that could not be told nor numbered for multitude.

1Kings 8:6 And the priests brought in the Ark of the covenant of the LORD unto his place, into the oracle of the house, to the most holy place, even under the wings of the cherubims.

1Kings 8:9 There was nothing in the Ark save the two tables of stone, which Moses put there at Horeb, when the LORD made a covenant with the children of Israel, when they came out of the land of Egypt.

Solomon has succeeded his father David as King over Israel and is tasked to build God a temple. His father hasn't been able to because He has been a Man of war throughout his lifetime. Solomon spends seven years in building this great edifice, throwing all his time and resources into it. God's house is finally complete and preparations are underway for opening day. His last assignment is now to fetch the Ark and holy vessels from the City of David into Jerusalem, their designated place. What transpired clues us in on how the Word of God ought to be shepherded into the place of our heart/spirit.

1.   Passion and Urgency.

Verse one opens with Solomon summoning all the elders, heads and chiefs of the children of Israel to fetch the Ark of the Covenant from the City of David into Jerusalem. I can imagine an atmosphere that is electric and full of anticipation. All through the seven years of building the Temple, he had waited and envisioned this day. With passion levels high and excitement in the air, he marshals his energies towards the cause of fetching the Ark of God from the City of David. His attitude and actions demonstrated passion and urgency on his part.

Child of God, like Solomon, you and I are supposed to have the passion that unashamedly moves us to freely talk about the beauty, benefits and blessedness of God's Word; with our families, friends, workmates and learn to speak it to ourselves as well. As your day begins, do you have the passion and inner urgency to open your Bible, read and hear what your King's marching orders for the day are? Do you see it befitting to tune in and listen to a Christian channel on your TV set, flipping past your favorite movie and football channels? Come Sunday

morning, do you get excited about Church and what your heavenly father has got to say to you?

Passion for His word begins and brings you to a place where you aren't ashamed of it. You learn to muse over it, mumble it, mutter it, to a point where your desire for it wells up in you and is visibly written on your face and lips. Friend, passion is paramount in the placement process.

2. Celebration.

The second verse goes on to say that all men assembled to Solomon at the feast. Solomon threw a party for the reception of the Ark. He couldn't help it but go into celebration mode when the Ark was making its way into Jerusalem. There was happiness and jubilation on his part; something he could not restrain. His title and position as King weren't going to deter or diminish his disposition. He knew it was God that had made him who he was and enabled him attained what he had. This was more reason for him to celebrate God for his faithfulness, goodness and mercy.

Andrew Allans Mutambo

A viable lesson for every child of God that God's Word in our lives should be celebrated at all times. It is encoded with His Will for you. It is forever true, faithful, powerful and dependable. All things pass away but His Word lasts forever. If we were to take a walk through the corridors of our minds into our past and recall the times His Word has been a lamp and light on to our feet and path. How it has always shielded and shepherded us from evil and destruction. This should provoke your heart into celebration for the Word, as you prepare to hear and receive it again into your life; because it does not return unto Him empty. As you diligently receive it, it triggers healing, deliverance, transformation, empowerment, blessings and protection. Thanks be to God!

3. Spiritual effort.

Notice in the third verse that there was effort on the part of the elders. They came and took up the Ark from the City of David, the town of Bethlehem unto Jerusalem. There ought to have been some reasonable distance between these two Cities nevertheless, their assignment outweighed their concerns. Remember, the priests had

to bear the Ark on their shoulders as protocol demanded. Similarly, there are things God will not do unless His children demonstrate a willingness to go an extra mile in pursuing His Word. Truth and revelation is valuable. Sometimes it may cost you moving out in the harshness of winter, chilliness of the night or heat of the day-to attend a Church service or gospel meeting.

While living in these physical bodies whose dictates are always contrary to our spirit man, there are things our 'flesh' will always try to compromise on or stop us from achieving. Excuses, procrastination, negative energy and attitudes will often surface when it's time to feed and exercise our spirit-man. This is when you begin downloading all the fatigue of the day; you feel sick, sleepy, tired, emotionally low and on.

Notwithstanding, this is also the time you need to take a stand by declaring, 'I don't walk by the flesh but by the Spirit'. It takes spiritual effort (your spirit taking the lead) to rise and go get the Ark (Word of God). Get up from bed, get a hold of your bible and go to the living room to read and meditate on it. This continuous exertion will silence and put the 'flesh' into mortification.

4. Sacrifice.

While the jubilation was ongoing, Solomon and the folks present at the feast decided to take the event a notch higher. They felt they needed to spice the event with sacrifices of sheep and oxen. We are told they began sacrificing sheep and oxen that could not be told in number. I can only imagine the burst of activity as the priests were totally overwhelmed with the influx of animals to be slaughtered on the altar. They beckoned their Levite brethren to join the exercise. The sacrifices were a massive display of affection and reverence to God.

Our sheer passion and gratitude for God's Word, leads us to easily and freely avail ourselves as living sacrifices. As the Word makes its way into the inner parts of our lives, we spontaneously respond to it by releasing and relinquishing those things and areas that we had held onto, the ones God is demanding and leading us to give up.

The Scripture says, Solomon offered 120,000 sheep and 22,000 oxen. I am not certain what percentage

came from the people; but I am sure the bulk was from Solomon. Wow, look at the sacrificial and giving heart! If as Christians we will realize that who we are and what we have has its genesis from Jesus the King, only then will we learn to let go into God's hands both the challenges and blessings of life. How many times has God told you to release something or someone but you have stubbornly refused and paid a deaf ear? You will notice that in the aftermath of Solomon's sacrifice, God appears to Him and rewards his later years. It's up to you to either hold on to, hold back OR release those few loaves and fish and you will enjoy the goodies that come with the sacrifice and obedience. The choice is yours.

Romans 12:1 I beseech you therefore, brethren, by the mercies of God, that ye present your bodies a living sacrifice, holy, acceptable unto God, which is your reasonable service.

5.   Fixation.

Towards the climax of the event, the Ark was safely guided into the Holy of Holies, its designated place. Solomon and his team had to follow divine etiquette governing the temple and its assets; and in this respect the Ark of the Covenant. As long as the Ark remained in the outer-court or in the middle court, the ceremony was inconclusive. There was no room for error, complacency or presupposition. Earlier on when David had not followed protocol, he lost one of his men (Uzzah). Solomon was careful not to fall into a similar fate. He had to follow procedure to the letter.

Solomon's temple was an archetype of the living temples made without hands, that Christ would build and establish through His finished work on Calvary. You and I are now the temples of God, the dwelling place of God's eternal Spirit. Like the physical temple was partitioned in three; outer-court, inner-court and inner most court, our lives comprise; the body (outer court), soul (inner court) and spirit (inner most court). It's in our spirit that the Ark (Word) settles. When we receive the Word via sermon or personal study, it registers onto our minds but is meant to settle in our spirit. In our mind, it deposits knowledge and on its way to our spirit, it becomes revelation. Knowledge is good and beneficial but revelation impacts your life. His Word is spirit and your spirit, is its rightful place of abode.

Psalms 119:11 Thy word have I hid in mine heart, that I might not sin against thee.

6.   Contents.

The ninth verse of our passage says there was nothing in the Ark except the two tables of stone Moses put there. On these were written the ten commandments given to the Children of Israel on Mount Sinai. In them God spelt out their duty to Him and to one's neighbor. They are a reflection of God's Word to us. His Word stipulates our obligations and God's promised blessings.

Since the contents of the Ark were solely the two tablets of stone, and serious care and caution was placed on it, it underscored its magnitude and value. The Word of God should be treated with utmost gravity, knowing that it stands alone, pure, and unadulterated. It should not be compared to or substituted with anything. Its contents should never be supplemented, subtracted or substituted in any way. Paul goes on to say, *Gal 1:8 But though we, or an angel from heaven, preach any other gospel unto you than that which we have preached unto you, let him be accursed.*

Therefore, as it makes its way to your spirit to find settlement, you should ask yourself, is what I'm embracing the pure and true gospel. Or am listening to what my feelings long to hear? Is what this preacher-man sharing sound doctrine? Or, as you study your Bible, is it speaking to you or you are filtering through your soul what your senses would want to hear?

Friends, our duty is to see to it that as we 'fetch' the Ark (Word) through personal /group study and sermon hearing, it's received and conceived in its purity and channeled to its **Place-which is your spirit.** This is level one in helping you understand the dynamics of His Word.

Chapter Two

Purpose of the Word.

As we continue our discussion about our scriptural text (John 1:1), let us examine another phrase, *"...and the Word was with God"*. Emphasis is going to be put on the preposition 'with'. The word 'with' literally means; in union, association, companionship, instrumentality. In relation to our subject, it means working together. The story of creation in the book of Genesis is our Father's hand book, teaching us the importance of working with His word in creating a wholesome world around us. Closer examination of the name God (Elohim), reveals the involvement of the three persons of the God-head. The name is in its plural, yet singular form.

Let us take a step back in the eon of time before creation and imagine it being total nothingness, except God

(Father, Living Word and Holy Spirit). The Godhead imagines life and an expansive creation and through the six days of creation, God gets to work. The Father's role was to speak as He drew from the wealthy resource of His Word (Christ) in Him. During the entire exercise, which was hustle free and without a sweat, He considered the Living Word (Christ) as a companion/work-mate to fashion the different aspects of life.

The Father and the Living Word literally worked together to create the universe we live in. It marvels me how the cosmos (inclusive of the planets that have been discovered and those that are not), came into existence through decree. Imagine God (Elohim-Father, Son and Holy Spirit) standing somewhere in eternity past and speaking. With every spoken word came its offspring. Outstanding, wasn't it?

Have you chanced to walk through thick jungles, rugged mountains OR flown over massive seas and gigantic deserts? Well, words are inadequate to describe the beauty, magnificence and greatness of some of these objects of creation. If you can be awe struck by His

creation, how much more their Creator? The point is, all this is a product of His Spoken Word.

Hebrews 11:3 Through faith we understand that the worlds were framed by the word of God, so that things which are seen were not made of things which do appear.

Genesis 1:1 In the beginning God created the heaven and the earth.

Genesis 1:2 And the earth was without form, and void; and darkness was upon the face of the deep. And the Spirit of God moved upon the face of the waters.

Genesis 1:3 And God said, Let there be light: and there was light.

Genesis 1:4 And God saw the light, that it was good: and God divided the light from the darkness.

Genesis 1:5 And God called the light Day, and the darkness he called Night. And the evening and the morning were the first day.

Genesis 1:6 And God said, Let there be a firmament in the midst of the waters, and let it divide the waters from the waters.

Genesis 1:7 And God made the firmament, and divided the waters which were under the firmament from the waters which were above the firmament: and it was so.

Genesis 1:8 And God called the firmament Heaven. And the evening and the morning were the second day.

Genesis 1:9 And God said, Let the waters under the heaven be gathered together unto one place, and let the dry land appear: and it was so.

Genesis 1:10 And God called the dry land Earth; and the gathering together of the waters called he Seas: and God saw that it was good.

Genesis 1:11 And God said, Let the earth bring forth grass, the herb yielding seed, and the fruit tree yielding fruit after his kind, whose seed is in itself, upon the earth: and it was so.

Genesis 1:12 And the earth brought forth grass, and herb yielding seed after his kind, and the tree yielding

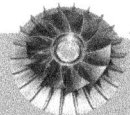

fruit, whose seed was in itself, after his kind: and God saw that it was good.

Genesis 1:13 And the evening and the morning were the third day.

Genesis 1:14 And God said, Let there be lights in the firmament of the heaven to divide the day from the night; and let them be for signs, and for seasons, and for days, and years:

Genesis 1:15 And let them be for lights in the firmament of the heaven to give light upon the earth: and it was so.

Genesis 1:16 And God made two great lights; the greater light to rule the day, and the lesser light to rule the night: he made the stars also.

Genesis 1:17 And God set them in the firmament of the heaven to give light upon the earth,

Genesis 1:18 And to rule over the day and over the night, and to divide the light from the darkness: and God saw that it was good.

Genesis 1:19 And the evening and the morning were the fourth day.

Genesis 1:20 And God said, Let the waters bring forth abundantly the moving creature that hath life, and fowl that may fly above the earth in the open firmament of heaven.

Genesis 1:21 And God created great whales, and every living creature that moveth, which the waters brought forth abundantly, after their kind, and every winged fowl after his kind: and God saw that it was good.

Genesis 1:22 And God blessed them, saying, Be fruitful, and multiply, and fill the waters in the seas, and let fowl multiply in the earth.

Genesis 1:23 And the evening and the morning were the fifth day.

Genesis 1:24 And God said, Let the earth bring forth the living creature after his kind, cattle, and creeping thing, and beast of the earth after his kind: and it was so.

Genesis 1:25 And God made the beast of the earth after his kind, and cattle after their kind, and ever thing that creepeth upon the earth after his kind: and God saw that it was good.

Let us fast forward to the New Testament era and glean first hand from our Master Jesus. The fourth chapters of the gospels of Matthew and Luke give us a direct approach of Jesus working with His Word in defeating and subduing our greatest foe, Satan. After his baptism and the Father's authentication of His call, He heads to the wilderness of Judea to have a quiet time to seek God in preparation for His earthly ministry. While there, He is encountered by Satan who on three occasions tries to seduce and side track him from His purpose. You will notice that on each instance, Jesus silences His foe by quoting Scripture. At no single time did He imagine out of anger and disgust to use a swear word, cry foul or cower into some rock crevice out of fear like some Christians do; simply because He knew the laws governing the spiritual world.

In the kingdom of God, His Word is Law. Like I said before, He rules, governs and administrates the affairs of the earth realm by it. The devil understands this well. What Jesus did was to work with His companion (the Written Word) under the direction of God's Spirit. The result was the subjugation and fleeing of His adversary.

He was able to draw from the wealth of the written Word (commandments) within Him, which he often read and heard on Sabbath in the Synagogue, as He was growing up. When he was encountered with a situation that warranted its usage, He simply drew from its wellspring in Him. The commandments he had heard and read had become his companion and friend. And all through his ministry when confronted by demon spirits, Pharisees and Sadducees who wanted to challenge him through the Law, He was always a step ahead. They discovered that He was well versed with the Law, something they so marveled about. It is the first thirty years of His life that defined his last three and a half years. Those long and silent years He spent internalizing the Word were pivotal during his later years.

We also are to treat His Word as a friend and 'work' with it in creating a wholesome world around us. Imagine coming to a place where you perceive and value the Word of God as a companion. This will change your perspective on how you hear and read it. It will make you want to spend more time in it through meditation and study. And as you do this, it will become more and more a part of your life, a friend that sticks closer than a brother! Our

indulgence in God's Word brings us to a place where its wisdom begins rubbing off on us.

Job 29:6 When I washed my steps with butter, and the rock poured me out rivers of oil;

The Word of God is our Great Physician's toolkit. Its surgical precision makes it a healer and transformer as it works its way into our body, soul and spirit. Like an anti-fungal OR anti-bacterial, it begins fighting against the intruding forces, repairing and replenishing the parts that have been depleted. It also goes ahead to inflict harm and destruction upon every diabolic work and influence. When you and I take time to diligently listen, read, meditate and speak it over our lives, it spontaneously goes to work by healing, transforming, delivering, restoring and renewing us; leaving every aspect of our 'houses' clean and garnished free of demonic activity. It also begins ferrying all the wonderful goodies that our heavenly father wills for us; health, peace, joy, prosperity, protection, power, long life and favor.

One of the oldest books in the Bible, the book of Job declares, 'you shall decree a thing and it shall be established'. The word 'decree' comes from a Hebrew root word, 'divide or decide'. And the word 'thing', comes from another Hebrew root word, 'promise or word'. In quintessence, the Scripture would read, 'you shall divide and decide a promise or Rhema word from God, and it shall be confirmed. Your dividing and deciding, is based on your continuous engagement of the Word as you speak it over and over into your life. The more you declare it, that is, dividing (breaking it into dissolvable particles), the more you are dispatching its broken down elements into the farthest and deepest recesses of your life. Then and only then will it be established.

Job 22:28 Thou shalt also decree a thing, and it shall be established unto thee: and the light shall shine upon thy ways.

Another Scripture quote in the book of Jeremiah says, 'because you speak this Word'! Watch this, it does not say because you speak your words, quote some Shakespeare phrase or something you picked from a wonderful Christian book.....NO! But because you speak this 'matter' or 'thing' from His Word, under the direction of the Holy Spirit, I'm going to make (bestow and grant) fire on the words you are speaking and it shall devour them. Oh my

goodness, ours is to only engage and make busy the Word of God and it will go to work on our behalf. What are you waiting for, put this book aside for a minute, get a hold of your sword and begin wielding it over every affair in your life that demands it.

Jeremiah 5:14 Wherefore thus saith the LORD God of hosts, Because ye speak this word, behold, I will make my words in thy mouth fire, and this people wood, and it shall devour them.

Our final reference is again drawn from the book of Jeremiah. God is pausing a question to you and me. He uses two metaphors to define His Word. *'Is not my word like a fire and a hammer'?* What comes to mind when you look at these two elements? Depending on their size and magnitude, when put to adequate use, their creative or destructive powers can be immense. When we as Christians understand the significance of God's Word, no 'rock' can remain un-shuttered and no thicket can continue unconsumed.

Jeremiah 23:29 Is not my word like as a fire? saith the LORD; and like a hammer that breaketh the rock in pieces?

I am enjoying this-wow. What a treasure we have in God's Word. From this moment forth, let your perception levels for the Word rise. The Word of God should be one of your greatest companions. *It is a lamp onto our feet and light on to our path.* Work with it as you forge your path of destiny. As you declare it, it will illuminate your path and before you realize, you are crossing insurmountable rivers, leaping over walls, traversing deserts and scaling mountains.

Isaiah 55:11 So shall my word be that goeth forth out of my mouth: it shall not return unto me void, but it shall accomplish that which I please, and it shall prosper in the thing whereto I sent it.

Mathew 24:35 Heaven and earth shall pass away, but my words shall not pass away.

2 Corinthians 1:20 For all the promises of God in him are yea, and in him Amen, unto the glory of God by us.

Chapter Three

Position of the Word

In our final chapter, our focus is on the last part of the verse, John 1:1 *'...and the Word was God'.* In here, the name God means a Deity. The Living Word was and is Deity. Earlier in our conversation, I stipulated that the Living Logos and the Written Logos are one, because the latter is a product of the former. It is His reason and logic. Therefore, if the Living Word was God, then His written Word automatically enjoys the same status as its source. Let us look at this Scripture for more insight.

Psalms 138:2 I will worship toward thy holy temple, and praise thy name for thy loving kindness and for thy truth: for thou hast magnified thy word above all thy name.

David has decided to make this particular day, one of praise and thanksgiving. Citing the previous chapter

(Psalms 137), he seems to have had his fill of making petitions and supplications. In the course of his fellowship with God in prayer, he makes a stunning remark, *'I will worship toward thy holy temple, and praise thy name for thy loving kindness and for thy truth: for thou hast magnified thy word above all thy name.'* The reason for his switch into praise-mode was the revelation he had of the Word of God while he was in prayer; hence choosing to magnify it above His name. The word magnified means, 'promoted, advanced, honored, lifted up, nourished, made larger and to exceed'.

David's inspiration and resultant outburst of praise for God's Word, sprung from a sneak peek he had of the King's heavenly palace and in it, he saw the sacred oracle placed in a position of supremacy and given a status exceeding that of His (God's) name. Amazingly, the all powerful name of Jesus has been exalted far above all principality, power, might, dominion and every other name in all spheres. In the heavens'- it is highly revered, in sheol or depths of the earth, it is trembled at AND on the earth realm, it is a stress-code/gate-pass to all desiring to connect with heaven. Notwithstanding, His Word, enjoys a greater hierarchical status.

The Library of Congress is the largest library in the world, with more than 155.3 million items on approximately 838 miles of bookshelves. The collections include more than 35 million books and other print materials, 3.4 million recordings, 13.6 million photographs, 5.4 million maps, 6.5 million pieces of sheet music and 68 million manuscripts.

The Library was founded in 1800, making it the oldest federal cultural institution in the nation. On August 24, 1814, British troops burned the Capitol building (where the Library was housed) and destroyed the Library's core collection of 3,000 volumes. On January 30, 1815-Congress_-approved_-the_-purchase_-of_-Thomas Jefferson's personal library of 6,487 books for $23,950.

The Library receives some 15,000 items each working day and adds approximately 11,000 items to the collections daily. The majority of the collections are received through the Copyright registration process, as the Library is home to the U.S. Copyright Office. Materials are also acquired through gift, purchase, other government agencies (state, local and federal), Cataloging in Publication (a prepublication arrangement with publishers) and exchange with libraries in the United States and abroad. Items not selected for the collections or other internal purposes are used in the Library's national and international exchange programs. Through these exchanges the Library acquires material that would not be available otherwise. The remaining items are made available to other federal agencies and are then available for donation to educational institutions, public bodies and nonprofit tax-exempt organizations in the United States.

Since 1962, the Library of Congress has maintained offices abroad to acquire, catalog and preserve library and research materials from countries where such materials are essentially unavailable through conventional acquisitions methods. Overseas offices in New Delhi (India), Cairo (Egypt), Rio de Janeiro (Brazil), Jakarta (Indonesia), Nairobi (Kenya) and Islamabad (Pakistan) collectively acquire materials from more than 60 countries and acquire materials on behalf of United States libraries participating in the Cooperative Acquisitions Program. The Library is also collaborating with institutions around the globe to develop a World Digital Library.

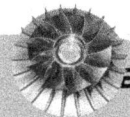

Imagine, every book that has been put in print and marketed in the United States, has a copy shelved in the library of Congress. That is why each book has its unique ISBN, this one too. In a similar manner, God has got the original copy of His Word eternally shelved in the throne room.

Psalms 119:89 Forever, O LORD, thy word is settled in heaven.

The above Scripture attests to its positioning. Settled means, 'established, stationed, set over, appointed and made to stand upright'. Its position is of a hierarchical nature which makes it; revere-able, powerful, indestructible, unchangeable and dependable. This elevated status means it is impregnable and supreme. No one can break through it, corrupt it, or manipulate it. And because it occupies a position of supreme authority and rank in the heavens, it's a dependable anchor whose legitimacy and faithfulness is un-questionable. The Word of God doesn't change OR falter. That is the reason you and I can refer to it, reflect on it, rehearse and release it into every aspect of our lives with outright surety.

Isaiah 66:2 For all those things hath mine hand made, and all those things have been, saith the LORD: but to this man will I look, even to him that is poor and of a contrite spirit, and trembleth at my word.

Let us take our conversation a notch higher. The preceding verse has told us that God will look to the person with this unique set of characteristics. The one who is poor, contrite and trembles at his Word. The word trembles means, 'afraid, fearful and reverential'. A detailed examination of this verse reveals that, in order to attract the favor and respect of God, it takes a lowly mind and humble spirit; which in turn produces the reverential fear for His Word. And because God places high premium on it, He is willing to reward all that are able to recognize its supreme status.

The Children of Israel have reached the borders of Canaan. The cherished Promised land is now in sight. They have seen and experienced the hostile wilderness the past forty years including the loss of an entire generation (most of whom were their parents and grandparents) through murmuring and unbelief. Moses now stands before this fresh generation and recapitulates the Law;

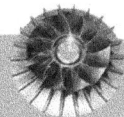

as he prepares to pass on the tools of government to his protégée Joshua. You will notice in this passage that they were placed on cross roads and given a mandate to choose which direction they would love to take. As long as they obeyed the commandments, the blessing was sure to come and the inverse if they took the nether path. Such was the worth and consequence YAHWEH God placed on the recipients of His Word.

Deuteronomy 11:26 Behold, I set before you this day a blessing and a curse;

Deuteronomy 11:27 A blessing, if ye obey the commandments of the LORD your God, which I command you this day:

Deuteronomy 11:28 And a curse, if ye will not obey the commandments of the LORD your God, but turn aside out of the way which I command you this day, to go after other gods, which ye have not known.

It is imperative that you and I perceive and treat God's Word like we would Him. This will give you a fresh outlook of it every other time you listen to and read it.

Conclusion

On the onset of this book, I did say that our focus will be on how the Word of God is received, conceived and released. We have looked at its place, purpose and position. In its three dimensional state, we have seen how it evolves from a 'mustard seed' that is dropped into our spirit, into a huge tree with deep roots, strong and enormous branches that offer shelter to many. This tree is a prototype of a life that has understood the operations of the Word of God. You can never comprehend the measure of greatness and influence a life that is engrossed in the Word of God can have.

Besides, God wants our lives to evolve from a weak, sick, defeated and beggarly mentality to that of an empowered and resourceful one, wholly governed by the dictates of His Word. A story is told of a leader of a company (100 soldiers) who comes to Jesus on behalf of his servant.

Given his military training and thinking, he implores Jesus for his servant's healing. In his narration, he perceives the command (word) Jesus would speak as a servant; that can be dispatched back and forth. His sheer faith and understanding of the operations of God's word occasioned him a miracle without Jesus' physical presence near the subject (ailing servant).

This passage comes to challenge us as Christians to remove the veil from our minds and enlarge our understanding of God and His Word. He is willing and able to do more than we can even ask or imagine, according to the power that resides in us.

Mathew 8:5 And when Jesus was entered into Capernaum, there came unto him a centurion, beseeching him,

Mathew 8:6 And saying, Lord, my servant lieth at home sick of the palsy, grievously tormented.

Mathew 8:7 And Jesus saith unto him, I will come and heal him.

Mathew 8:8 The centurion answered and said, Lord, I

am not worthy that thou shouldest come under my roof: but speak the word only, and my servant shall be healed.

Mathew 8:9 For I am a man under authority, having soldiers under me: and I say to this man, Go, and he goeth; and to another, Come, and he cometh; and to my servant, Do this, and he doeth it.

Mathew 8:10 When Jesus heard it, he marvelled, and said to them that followed, Verily I say unto you, I have not found so great faith, no, not in Israel.

In addition, each of us like Ezekiel the prophet has been assigned a valley to fix. Some valleys are huge and harsh. Notwithstanding, like Ezekiel spoke as he was commanded, we are to do likewise. Remember the wellspring of the Word should emanate from within you. Believe you me, we are going to see things falling in place; marriages, finances, dreams and health. The catch is learning and understanding the principles of the Word in its three dimensional nature.

Ezekiel 37:7 So I prophesied as I was commanded: and as I prophesied, there was a noise, and behold a shaking, and the bones came together, bone to his bone.

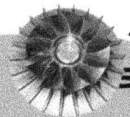

Ezekiel 37:8 And when I beheld, lo, the sinews and the flesh came up upon them, and the skin covered them above: but there was no breath in them.

Ezekiel 37:9 Then said he unto me, Prophesy unto the wind, prophesy, son of man, and say to the wind, Thus saith the Lord GOD; Come from the four winds, O breath, and breathe upon these slain, that they may live.

Ezekiel 37:10 So I prophesied as he commanded me, and the breath came into them, and they lived, and stood up upon their feet, an exceeding great army.

I wish you all God speed as you pass through your valley of Baca (weeping), and turn it into a spring. God bless!

Other Books written by Andrew Allans Mutambo:

1. Four Faces of a Worshipper.
2. Worship Keys.
3. Gates of Worship.
4. Purpose of praise.
5. Principles of Faith.

Coming Soon:

1. Seven Significances of the Cross.
2. Seven Locks of the Anointing.
3. Seven Characteristics of Prayer.
4. Nine Elements of Worship.
5. Composition of Worship.

www.ingramcontent.com/pod-product-compliance
Lightning Source LLC
Chambersburg PA
CBHW080533030426
42337CB00023B/4718